Growing Up
On A
New Hampshire
Pond

Joseph I Doran

I would like to dedicate
this book to my six grandchildren;
Taylor, Duncan, Griffin, Finnian, Alexander and Farrah.

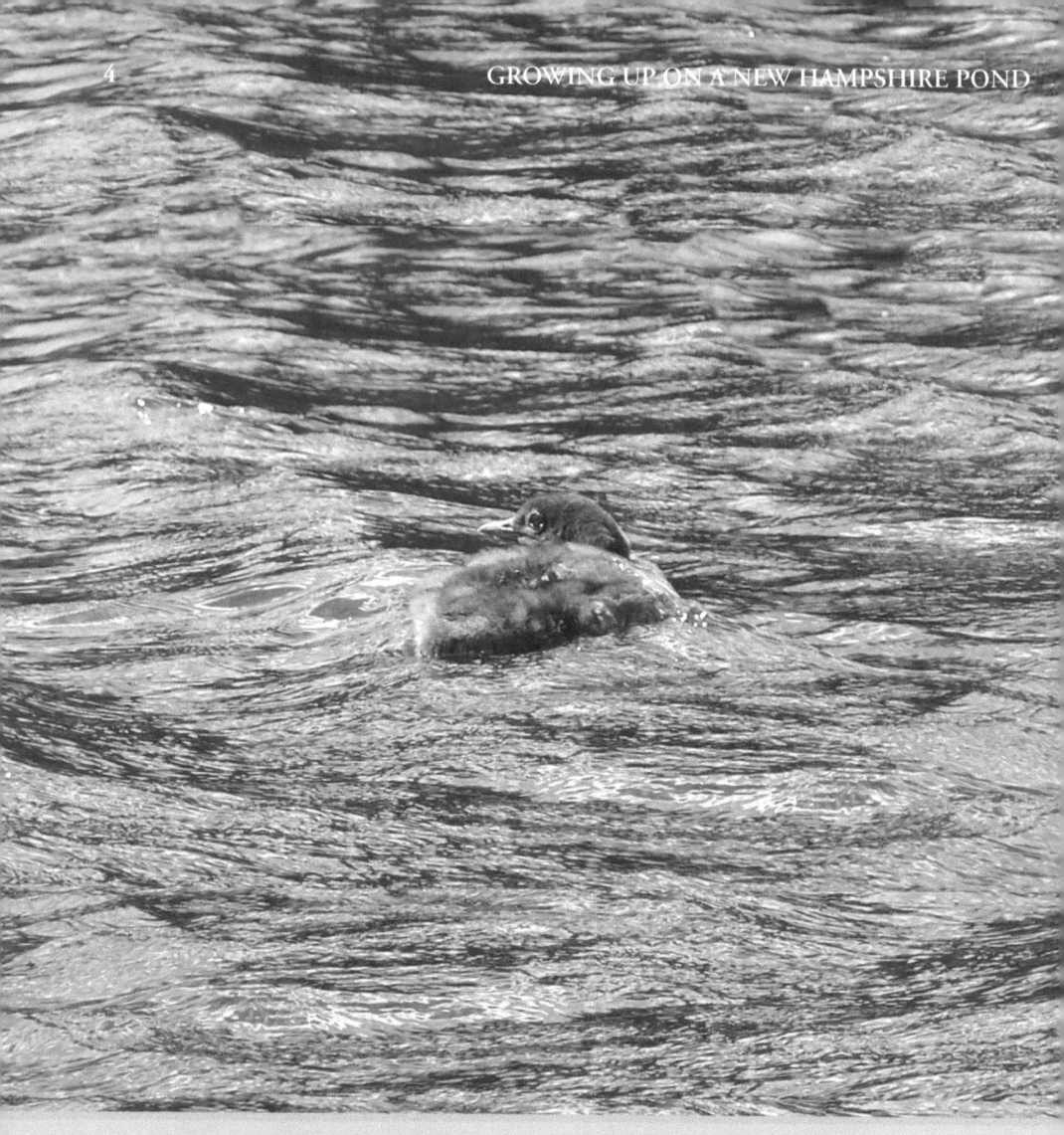

Hi, I am Jamie.

I'm a baby loon and I live with my Mommy and Daddy on a beautiful New Hampshire Pond.

This is my story.

This is my Mommy. She is sitting on her nest.

This is Daddy and he is
guarding the area around the
nest.

In mid-May, Mommy laid my egg and for the next 29 days she and Daddy took turns sitting on my egg.

I hatched on June 14. Within an hour Mommy had cleaned and dried me and plopped me in the water.

I was a natural swimmer from the start. I was diving a few days later.

Those first few weeks I relied totally on Mommy and Daddy for everything: food, comfort, and protection.

When I got tired, I rested on Mommy's back. It was so warm and comfortable. I felt quite safe.

I am now a month old. I spend all my time with Mommy and Daddy, learning as I go.

As you can see, I have lost my black fluff and have replaced it with this brown plumage.

It is six weeks and I have earned some time by myself. This is the first time I've been away from Mommy and Daddy. I like it. I can dive and swim under water very well. I'm starting to fish for myself, now.

It is mid-August and I am two months old. I now have my first year colors. My diving and swimming under water are getting better and better. Catching fish is another story.

My wings are developing
rapidly. With exercise, they get
stronger each day.

I want to fly!

HURRAY!!! I just caught my very own fish. It was delicious. Mom and Dad still provide most of my food, but I am getting better.

Part of growing up is learning to keep myself clean. This is called preening.

It is September and I can take care of myself now. Mom and Dad are still around for me, but I catch most of my fish. Most important, I can fly now. At three months I'm a young adult.

The season is changing: days are shorter, the water is cooler, and the trees are changing color.

The trees are not the only things changing color. Mom and Dad are changing color – to their winter colors. Mom says, "Jamie, in a few weeks we will look just like you."

October brings more changes. Dad left the other day. Mom said, "He has gone to winter fishing waters. We will follow him in a few weeks."

Mom looks a lot like me now.

Mom left for winter waters at the ocean, today. Now I am alone. It is the middle of November and it is getting cold. Ice is forming in shallow parts of the pond. The fishing is still good, so I'll stay a while longer. I will follow Mom soon.

It is early December and the pond is frozen over. Jamie is gone now, gone to the ocean to join Mom, Dad and all the other loons.

HAPPY FISHING JAMIE!

www.ingramcontent.com/pod-product-compliance
Lightning Source LLC
Chambersburg PA
CBHW050800290526
45792CB00008B/2258